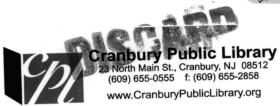

MAKING A
MOVIE

BY NADIA HIGGINS

AMICUS | AMICUS INK

Sequence is published by Amicus and Amicus Ink
P.O. Box 1329, Mankato, MN 56002
www.amicuspublishing.us

Library of Congress Cataloging-in-Publication Data
Names: Higgins, Nadia, author.
Title: Making a movie / by Nadia Higgins.
Description: Mankato, MN : Amicus/Amicus Ink, [2019] | Series: Sequence. Entertainment |
 Includes bibliographical references and index.
Identifiers: LCCN 2017049063 (print) | LCCN 2017049597 (ebook) | ISBN 9781681515236
 (pdf) | ISBN 9781681514413 (library binding) | ISBN 9781681523613 (pbk.)
Subjects: LCSH: Cinematography--Juvenile literature.
Classification: LCC TR851 (ebook) | LCC TR851 .H54 2019 (print) | DDC 777--dc23
 LC record available at https://lccn.loc.gov/2017049063

Editor: Wendy Dieker
Book Designer: Ciara Beitlich and Veronica Scott
Photo Researcher: Holly Young

Photo Credits: Jiri Hera/Shutterstock cover; VektorSport/Shutterstock cover; George Rudy/
Shutterstock 4–5; oliver leedham/Alamy 6–7; ASDF_Media/Shutterstock 8–9; A.F. Archive/Alamy
10–11; Hill Street Studios/Getty 12–13; Marco Saroldi/Shutterstock 14–15; Caspar Benson
/ fStop Images GmbH/Alamy 16–17; Pavel Losevsky/Dreamstime 18–19; Hanna Zelenko/
WikiCommons 20–21; Ingram Publishing/Newscom 22–23; Gorodenkoff/Shutterstock 24–25;
Robert Daly/iStock 26–27; andresr/iStock 28–29

Printed in China

HC 10 9 8 7 6 5 4 3 2 1
PB 10 9 8 7 6 5 4 3 2 1

A Good Movie Idea

Every movie begins with an idea. Zombie dogs? Evil clowns? Magical underwear? A **producer** is always thinking about movie ideas. Their job is to find one that will be a hit.

That great idea could come from a book. A news story could spark it. A writer could say, "Hey, I have an idea!"

Many movies are based on published books. What's your favorite book? Would it make a good movie?

LOADING...LOADING...LOADING...

INTERCUT - INT. LOCATION #1/LOCATION #2 - DAY

If it's necessary to CUT back and forth between
simultaneous action in two different locations in the same
scene, then handle your scene heading like this. Use this
method when you want to show a phone conversation.

                    CHARACTER #1
              (into phone)
        You can then type your dialogue as
        normal.

                    CHARACTER #2
              (into phone)
        Whilst indicating that both
        characters are on the phone.

                    CHARACTER #1
              (into phone)
        Just make sure you indicate when
        the character hangs up.
              (hangs up)
        Especially if you are going to
        continue the dialogue and scene
        beyond the phone conversation.

   LOCATION #1 - DAY

   natively, you can establish both location

                       CHARACTER #1
              (into phone) character speaking
        Show your first character speaking
        into the phone like this

**Actors highlight their
lines in a script.**

The script is written.

...LOADING...LOADING...

What about alien worms? That's it! The producer hires a screenwriter to write the **script**. They call it *Slime on Earth*.

A movie script is like a big book. It maps out everything about the movie. It tells who the characters are. It explains where each scene happens. It shows what the actors will say, word for word.

It is time to **pitch** the script to a movie studio. A studio is in the business of making movies. But first, the producer finds a director. This person will be in charge of creative decisions.

Great news! A huge movie star wants to play a worm chaser. That makes the pitch go even better. *Slime on Earth* is a go!

The movie studio executive likes the script! He tells the producers to start working on the movie.

The script is written.

YEAR 1 →

DING . . . LOADING . .

Movie studio accepts the script; producers get to work making the movie.

An artist draws a storyboard. Now the team will know what the movie will look like.

The script is written.

Designers work on storyboard, set plans, and costumes.

. . . L O A D I N G . .

Movie studio accepts the script; producers get to work making the movie.

Preproduction

There is so much to plan. This time is called **preproduction**. A **storyboard** is drawn. This looks like a comic book. It shows what each camera shot will look like.

The **sets** are sketched, too. Some scenes will take place on the alien planet. Someone needs to design the costumes too. The whole creative team is busy during preproduction.

Meanwhile, actors line up at the studio. They have come to try out for the roles. They practice reading from the script. A hundred actors may read for the part of Screaming Teenager.

Who gets picked? Actors with talent, for sure. Sometimes two actors "click." They work so well together that they both get hired.

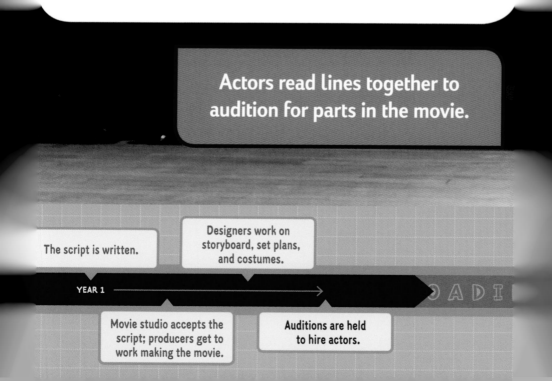

Actors read lines together to audition for parts in the movie.

The script is written.

Designers work on storyboard, set plans, and costumes.

YEAR 1

Movie studio accepts the script; producers get to work making the movie.

Auditions are held to hire actors.

The script is written.

Designers work on storyboard, set plans, and costumes.

The producers plan props and staff, map out the schedule, and figure out costs.

YEAR 1

N G . . .

Movie studio accepts the script; producers get to work making the movie.

Auditions are held to hire actors.

The staff works out more details. What equipment will be used? **Prop** designers are working on robotic worms. This movie stars a heroic dog, so an animal trainer needs to be hired, too.

How much will this all cost? How long will filming take? The producer sets the budget. She makes sure there is a schedule.

Filming a scene outdoors requires lots of equipment and many people.

LOADING . . . LOADING . . . LOADING . . .

Action!

At last, filming can begin. Hundreds of people get to work at once. The crew sets up lights and cameras. Hair and makeup artists get to work. They spend hours turning one actor into an alien.

The actors go on set. The director figures out where everybody will stand and how they will move. This is called **blocking**.

The script is written.

Designers work on storyboard, set plans, and costumes.

The producers plan props and staff, map out the schedule, and figure out costs.

YEAR 1 ⟶ YEAR 2

Movie studio accepts the script; producers get to work making the movie.

Auditions are held to hire actors.

Filming begins.

The director watches from the side. He helps the actors bring their roles to life.

PROD.
ROLL
B
SCENE
1F
TAKE
3
DIRECTOR:
CAMERA:
DATE:
07. 12. 2010
Day Nite Int Ext Mos
Filter
Sync

DIRECTOR

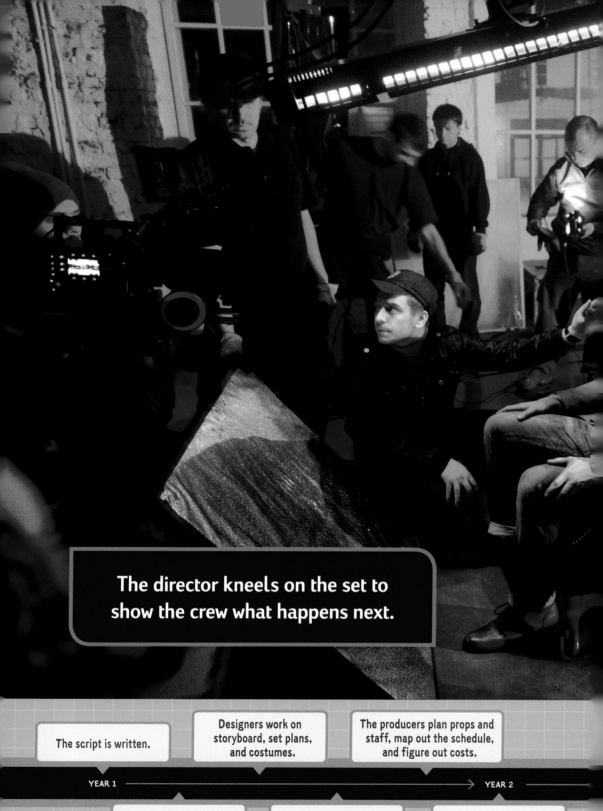

The director kneels on the set to show the crew what happens next.

The script is written.

Movie studio accepts the script; producers get to work making the movie.

Designers work on storyboard, set plans, and costumes.

Auditions are held to hire actors.

The producers plan props and staff, map out the schedule, and figure out costs.

Filming begins.

YEAR 1

YEAR 2

The director is not happy. The lights are too soft. The shadows should be darker. After all, this is a scary scene. The director wants the camera lowered, too. Filming from below will make the scene look creepier.

At last, the director is ready. Everyone is quiet. "Roll camera! Roll sound! Action!"

Filming continues.

The cameras roll for just a minute. The actors say their lines. "Cut!" The first **take** is done. But one of the actors wants to start over. Roll again. This scene could have several takes.

Shooting a film is hard work. Days run long. Sometimes tired actors lose their tempers. When filming ends, everyone is ready to celebrate. They throw a **wrap party**.

An actor waits next to the camera for her turn in the scene.

The script is written.

Designers work on storyboard, set plans, and costumes.

The producers plan props and staff, map out the schedule, and figure out costs.

YEAR 1   YEAR 2

Movie studio accepts the script; producers get to work making the movie.

Auditions are held to hire actors.

Filming begins.

Wrap party!

DING . . . LOADING . .

Filming continues.

The script is written.

Designers work on storyboard, set plans, and costumes.

The producers plan props and staff, map out the schedule, and figure out costs.

YEAR 1 ⟶ YEAR 2

Movie studio accepts the

Auditions are held

Filming begins.

Putting It All Together

The movie was filmed out of order. Scenes were shot based on where they took place. For example, Scenes 1 and 7 both happened in a corn field. It made sense to film them on the same day.

The film editor puts the movie in order. With the director, she also chooses the best takes.

The editor and her team pick the best takes. They put the film together.

Wrap party!

...LOADING...

Filming continues.

Film is edited.

23

Next, the sound editor gets to work. The crashing sound of breaking glass is added in. Now comes the scary music.

Scene 3 still needs an animated flying spaceship, though. Computers are used to add in the special effect. Last of all come the **credits**. They show the names of all the people who worked on the movie.

An animator uses a computer to add in special effects.

The script is written.

Designers work on storyboard, set plans, and costumes.

The producers plan props and staff, map out the schedule, and figure out costs.

YEAR 1

YEAR 2

Movie studio accepts the script; producers get to work making the movie.

Auditions are held to hire actors.

Filming begins.

Wrap party!

Sound and computer graphics are added.

Filming continues.

Film is edited.

Now Showing

Meanwhile, the movie's **trailer** is showing in theaters. This one-minute teaser leaves viewers wanting more. Huge movie posters line movie theater windows.

All the movie's stars show up for the **movie premiere**. They look so glamorous for this first showing. Fans can hardly wait to see it for themselves!

The script is written.

Designers work on storyboard, set plans, and costumes.

The producers plan props and staff, map out the schedule, and figure out costs.

YEAR 1 ⟶ YEAR 2

Movie studio accepts the script; producers get to work making the movie.

Auditions are held to hire actors.

Filming begins.

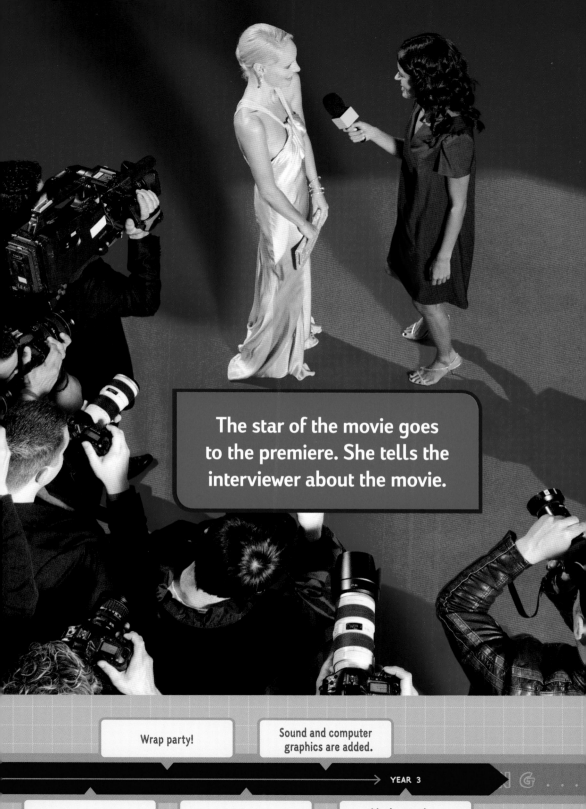

The star of the movie goes to the premiere. She tells the interviewer about the movie.

Wrap party!

Sound and computer graphics are added.

YEAR 3

Filming continues.

Film is edited.

Movie premiere takes place.

The script is written.

Designers work on storyboard, set plans, and costumes.

The producers plan props and staff, map out the schedule, and figure out costs.

YEAR 1 ⟶ YEAR 2

Movie studio accepts the script; producers get to work making the movie.

Auditions are held to hire actors.

Filming begins.

It is opening weekend—at last! The movie is showing at thousands of theaters. Fans line up out the door for tickets. After working for three years, the producer, director, and hundreds of crew members hope fans will love *Slime on Earth*.

A family goes to see the new movie. The movie studio hopes they love it.

Wrap party!	Sound and computer graphics are added.	The finished movie opens at theaters!

YEAR 3

Filming continues.	Film is edited.	Movie premiere takes place.

GLOSSARY

block To plan out where the actors will stand and move.

credits The list of the names of all the people who helped make the movie.

movie premiere A special showing of a movie for the stars, crew, and their guests.

pitch To sell an idea for a movie.

preproduction The stage in a movie-making when people finalize the script, plan costumes, create storyboards of the shots, hire actors, and plan filming locations.

producer A person who guides a movie from start to finish, especially when it comes to business decisions.

prop An object used on set.

script A book that tells everyone who is in the movie, what the actors will say, and where the movie will take place.

set The scenery and furniture that makes up the pretend world of a movie stage.

storyboard A series of drawings that show what the movie's shots will look like.

take One filming of a scene.

trailer An ad for a movie.

wrap party A party for the cast and crew after filming is completed.

READ MORE

Baggaley, Ann, ed. *The Children's Book of Movies: Explore the Magical, Behind-the-Scenes World of the Movies.* New York: DK Publishing, 2014.

Hammelef, Danielle S. *Epic Stunts.* North Mankato, Minn.: Capstone Press, 2015.

Spence, Kelly. *Get Into Claymation.* New York: Crabtree Publishing, 2017.

WEBSITES

Arthur: Buster's Sad Movie
http://pbskids.org/arthur/games/moviemaker/moviemaker.html

Behind the Scenes of the LEGO Batman Movie
https://www.dk.com/us/explore/lego/behind-the-scenes-of-the-lego-batman-movie-how-it-was-made/

wikiHow to Write a Simple Screenplay (for Kids)
http://www.wikihow.com/Write-a-Simple-Screenplay-(for-Kids)

INDEX

ABOUT THE AUTHOR

Nadia Higgins has been editing and writing books for 20 years. She has published more than 100 books for kids and teens. Nadia's favorite part of the job is doing research. She uses all kinds of media, from TV shows to podcasts, to find the best facts for her books.

CRANBURY PUBLIC LIBRARY

23 North Main Street

Cranbury, NJ 08512

609-655-0555

cranburypubliclibrary.org